51

Golden Pieces

BlueInk
SCRIBBLE

51
Golden
Pieces

Jean René Bazin PierrePierre

Table of Contents

Preamble

On the avenue one summer day, as I sat in my car, waiting for a friend,
I watched a mother get off her car, some ten feet away.
She got to the back door, reached inside the car to help out a young
child from his car seat. She stood him next to her on the sidewalk.
He must have been no more than four years old, restless and
turbulent, as they can be at that age.
All of a sudden, the young boy started sprinting down the sidewalk. At
first she didn't notice the action as she was reaching for something else
inside the car. But then she realized that the boy was not next to her.
The kid dashed on the sidewalk, passed a few pedestrians window
shopping and headed for the intersection. The petrified mother
desperately screamed for help but the vibrant street life drowned her
vocal efforts. The kid did not slow down but rather went straight into
the traffic. His little speedy legs, pounding on the asphalt, took him
straight into the street. He stopped for some reason, probably having
heard the mother's voice. As he turned around to look in her direction,
he noticed that truck heading straight at him. There, terrified, frozen,
as it seemed, he covered his eyes with his little hands. In his four-year-
old mind, maybe that was the surest way to make
the truck disappear... So sad, huh!
Was the truck driver paying attention or was picking from his lap,
at that same exact instant, some of the chips he was having,
snacking on...?

Foreword

This Love

An intelligent, discreet and pious young woman
Is worth more than all the money in the world.
Tell her that you love her more than your life,
Because this present life is nothing,
And that your only hope is that the two of you pass
Through this life in such a way that,
In the world to come,
You will be united in perfect love.

St John Chrysostom

Cathy's Theme

Day after day our love grows,
Day after day our fondness shows.
We did not plan any of this
But still could not pretend to miss
The craving for each other's voice,
The calls for which we had no choice.

It all started so quietly,
It all started kindly, softly.
And yet steadily, like the spring
With flowers one by one budding,
Love made over our stern faces,
Sweeping of our fears all traces.

Funny how much I think of you
In my many chores all day through.
Funny how the sound of your voice
Can hush in my world any noise.
Though blessings we receive many,
We should cheer when they're uncanny.

Day after day this our love grows,
The heart catches what the soul throws.
So soon before I see your eyes,
Love's flame will have doubled in size.
And as you reap just what you sow,
Surely, strongly this love will grow.

Our Time

There'll be a time for me and you
When love will come back to settle
All accounts so long overdue,
When fears were still kind and gentle.

There'll be a time for me and you
When hand in hand we'll have the choice
To grieve over what we've been through
Or for our gained wisdom rejoice.

There'll be a time for me and you
For then wrapped up in Nature's arms
We will savor what is so true;
The treasures of our inner charms.

There'll be a time for me and you
That will stifle all the false hopes,
That crush hearts, bodies and souls too,
Setting a stage for us to mope.

So here's the time for me and you.
Daffodils and lilacs galore
Adorning the stage for us two
To perform love just as before.

Rise and Shine

To wake up each and every day
To the sultry sound of your voice,
That chases all bad dreams away,
And of my fears stifles the noise.

To watch you sip your first coffee
With your blank eyes still full of dreams,
Your hair fixed up like a trophy,
Ever-strong rampart for your schemes.

You try painfully to wake up
And all your gestures amuse me
Even the prayer muffled up
Seems to dispel my misery.

I would take a lengthy pleasure
Washing you down in the shower.
Your skin silky beyond measure
Tenderly pat dry thereafter.

But if I would tell you all this
Really you'd never understand
That despite all my cheap follies
Without you I just would not stand

God knows if deep inside you too
Experience the same dilemma
Then in this case slowly us two
Will overcome all these dramas.

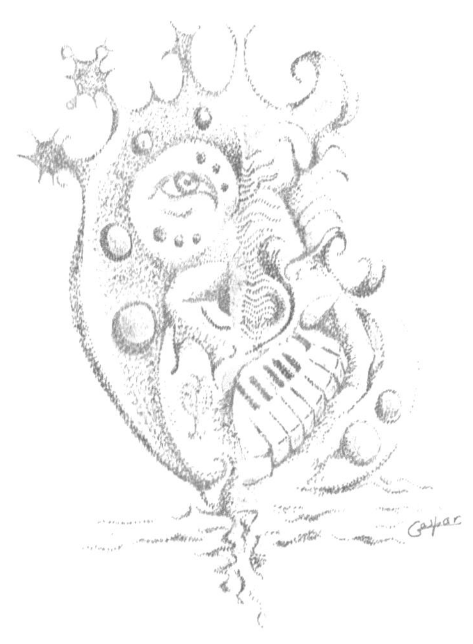

Insight

In flowery meadows of my mind,
You pace lightly, pace silkily,
The flowery meadows that I find
When thoughts of you come down swiftly.

In the spring valley of my heart
You run solely, so steadily,
The spring valley that would infarct
If far from me you would journey.

But in the kingdom of my soul
Your name shine on every banner.
Against all odds we will grow old
With blessed peace as a treasure.

So it is

A poem will say it plain,
A poem will say it all.
It's sweet as a refrain
But loud as a clear call.

It's a song with no beat
Set up to stand alone.
No need to move your feet
To its uncanny tone.

So often it reveals
What we seem to forget.
Genuine souls it can thrill,
Loving hearts it can pet.

Grab the weight of each word,
The stead of every rhyme,
The cry often unheard,
The truths that shun all time…

Woe to whosoever
Ignores what it conveys.
Their plans are forever
Doomed not to see the day.

So a poem hits and runs
Moving to the next friend
Begging them that they learn
The lessons close at hand.

A poem therefore will stain
The hearts of the many
Who luckily obtain
The wisdom it carries.

As I Say

The things I say are not so new,
The things I say are déjà vu.
The things I say I just repeat
As encore to hungry spirits.

The things I say sometimes offend
Potential foes, potential friends.
The things I say therefore remain
Or cause of joy or cause of pain.

The things I say therefore will be
Ringing in the ears of many.
The things I say are here to stay
For nothing's worth… the things I say.

A Season's Revenge

Some of you in chorus rejoiced
When the trees came budding anew.
From the arctic I heard the voice
Of the crowd cheering all day through.

The fewsome who truly missed me
Kept in their hearts their mourning veil.
They hoped and prayed that the balmy
Degrees were soon to no avail.

For the majority ignored
That never a season expires.
It may be delayed or enchored
But always return much dire.

I will make you regret the days
When the weather was warm and sweet,
At times you will wish you had stayed
Bundled safely between your sheets.

I come with wind just to inflict
To the land a bitter lesson;
Despite what the sky might depict,
One never buries a season.

The blanket I'll spread all over
Will linger, linger on the ground.
It will remain just to cover
Any object and any sound.

And so woe to whosoever
Will be caught outside choring,
My frigid degrees will hover
To traumatize all living things.

Even the groundhog you consult
Will remain baffled by the shock
Resulting straight from the insult,
A season by the whole world mocked.

And so winter is back in force
By some twist of nature, revived.
It returned riding a white horse
And wants to change all the archives,

Self-declaring to be the first
Winter expected for so long
Yet to deliver such a burst
Of air so cold and winds so strong.

Newtown, CT/Uvalde, TX

…And suddenly with no warning they flew.
They departed, like birds so often do.
They left the earth with all its promises,
They even shun all our hugs and kisses.

They traded all for the great other side.
There they will play and never have to hide.
They will know love like humans never do
And like angels they'll pray for me and you.

For willingly one of those days they came,
All full of love but with no one to blame.
They wanted to, loaded with human charm,
Simply invite the country to disarm.

Their sacrifice, horrific as it seems,
Should in us all get rid of any scheme.
For suddenly, like martyrs often do
They laid their lives so that we won't have to.

Alone

And so alone I stand,
Alone, with empty hand,
Alone without a dream
Thinking it's just a scheme
The silent one in me
Feeds me repeatedly.

Alone, no one to vent,
Fearing I may repent
From seeing their faces,
Or hearing faint traces
Or worries they'd harbor
When faced with my candor.

Alone, facing my fears,
Alone, wiping my tears,
When unannounced you come
And make my mind your home.
Alone, my heart in trance
Begging for one more chance.

Alone, oh so alone
But polishing the throne
That my heart, though captive
Has lovingly conceived
For you I so adore,
You, I yearn and pine for.

And so alone I'll stay,
In silence beg and pray
For the twin of my soul
To come and pay the toll
To this love tearing me
And at least set me free.

14

Aspects of Love

To finally fathom that in this misery
We call life you're the one tailor-made just for me,
To feel the world crumble at the mere glimpse of thought
That the queen of my world you've chosen to be not,
It's the irony of love.

To want to offer you the bestest of my years,
To shoulder all your loads, to wipe away your tears.
To be the one you search when your sun does not shine,
And in good and bad times still be yours while you're mine;
It's the promise of love.

To fall in love again at every glance you hush,
To yearn for your sweet words; but then you don't say much. To trail
around with you while you do your errands
And decipher meanwhile your subtle love demands;
It's just the plight of love.

To hold my very breath awaiting your verdict
And hear repeatedly that I will not be picked,
To beg and plead my case, your heart turned into stone,
And sadly realize that I have been dethroned;
It's the cruelty of love.

To come to your abode with my heart on my sleeve
Just to prove you my love and your sweet hand retrieve.
To notice in your voice a hope for tomorrow
That reveals that you will take away my sorrow;
It's just the joy of love.

Barclay Avenue

Caught in the stillness of my night
I see your face.
And since my thoughts so far are bright
I found erased
All the worries of my today;
They magically just fade away.

It's always the same scenario.
First you appear then the ratio
That you generate with the zeal
Caused by you fondling my heart still.

You are my light in darkest days,
You are the bright sun of my rays,
You are the soul I'll be searching
Long, long, after my life ending.

So don't ask that I should forget
What we once had.
I still love my darling "Hornet",
Color me mad…
You magically just chase away
All my worries of any day.

Bequeathed

So now it seems that finally
My Christmas gift I have received.
She has come to me naturally
And none of my hopes has deceived.

Who would have thought in my lifetime,
Who would have thought, no one could tell,
Who would have thought that Christmas chime
Would one day sound like wedding bell?

For joyfully, O joyfully,
Hand in hand we walked in the church
At this midnight mass happily,
Our loving bond was felt so much.

And merrily and merrily,
In life we'll go singing His praise,
Since to us He gave all freely
This love that nothing can erase…

O my baby, my sweet princess,
Do you like me suffer the snare
Snuggling my heart that you harness,
Each time I see your face so fair?

For finally, so finally
I have received my Christmas gift
Delivered to me naturally,
Rare pearl, this Holy Night, bequeathed.

Birthday Queen

Today is such a lovely day,
Today brings about your birthday.
Today you will, as it should be,
Reign over the world, my baby.

And I, the servant, happily,
Wants to convey wishes many.
Since in my world you mean so much
I will offer my heart as such:

I wish you your heart's desires,
May God sustain all its fires
And feed you hope along the road
And always lighten up your load.

You remain to me the treasure
Handed down from all His creatures
To walk along the trail with me;
And so I cherish you baby.

Bitterings

I told myself so many times before
To shut the door and wait for nothing more.
I had my chance but in my ignorance
I senselessly refused her the last dance.

So now it seems I became a bit wise
This heavy fog's been lifted from my eyes.
I see clearly just what she meant to me
And without her just what my life will be.

I begged out loud the good Lord I treasure,
In His mercy, to restore my measure.
I cried out loud facing my loneliness,
Always tasting of her hands the caress.

Day after day I carry this burden.
Within my ears the voice of her, remains.
Within my heart, her love that I long for
Depicts my life in senseless metaphors.

I go through life so full of lovely shades
Of emotions as in joyful parades
But within me one color always stays;
A taunting gloom turning my world to gray.

And so it is that I long for her hand
Though many tears ever between us stand.
I'd give my life for a glimpse at her face,
I'd give the world to my mistake erase.

You hear stories of dead-end love affairs
But you never fathom the hearts they tear,
The many lives that slowly they stifle,
Even the souls that they leave all baffled.

The lowest point of my life will remain
That sad instant she walked into that train.
I stood there still sizing the anarchy
That rapidly swan dove right within me.

And ever since that heart-wrenching hour
I taste my life so bitter and sour.
My inner drive she took to who knows where
Leaving me pain and impending despair,

I will treasure every mem'ry of her
And call her name in my dreams whenever.
She will always reign on this lonely heart
Though in her flight she took its major part.

I beg of you please, go remind my son
That what you do you fail to get back none.
Unselfish love and faithful devotion
Are of this life the joyful solution.

Then I remind myself as an encore
To shut the door and wait for nothing more.
Though chances are, despite my ignorance
One blessed day I will find deliverance.

Call Me

One day you will arise and conceive that for you
Things that you planned ahead so much did not come true.
Remember that somewhere, under the same blue sky,
Beats a heart, breathes a soul to whom you said goodbye.

On that day you'll wake up and feel that bitter taste
That what you think was sure was indeed picked in haste
And will wish you had not, although so hard you tried,
Stifled this love inside and listened to your pride.

Then call me who in vain tried to forget the pain
You inflicted my heart wanting to love again.
Life is made of surprise and when you expect naught
There is always a rain after a lasted drought.

I promise to fulfill your deepest fantasies,
I'll bring you rare flowers, you said you like daisies.
If ever in my heart I would take my last sigh,
I would pray to the Lord to keep on you His eye.

But if instead the Lord, with many unveiled plans,
Would call upon you first, leaving my empty hands,
I'd go around the world with my cross down the path
Of life slowly dying, missing my other half.

Daily Thoughts

Just like this year lilacs, stroked by the daring sun,
Whispering to the spring that its time is at hand,
The thoughts of you gently come ashore on my mind.

They come and gently lie exposing their tan buns,
Well aware of the seal they once lovingly brand'
On my soul they possess, the soul you left behind.

Someone spoke of recess; of this they give me none.
They're cherished and pampered so they treasure the sand,
This sand yearning for you, all dejected and pined.

So like this year lilacs, rendered bold by the sun,
I cry out to you, this no one understands,
When thoughts of you, daily come and dock on my mind.

Divine Touch

It's 2 am and as usual,
Alone in my room I brainstorm,
The dawn is stillborn but casual,
Nothing is out of the norm.

So normally you step right in,
With no warning but with great ease.
Since of my world you are the queen,
Then naturally I feel so pleased.

I can tell you with a few words
The shiver of soul experienced
But the truth will never be heard
Until you ponder its essence.

You are the clear and new mirror
Of the love I get from my Lord,
By far His sole ambassador,
Bearer of love and care galore.

You will always come nudge my soul
Despite the long miles between us,
The blessing bestow made us whole
Although the bond is not obvious.

Eve of Love

Come and step right into my life
For you I've left the door ajar,
Come sweet angel and be my wife
I've known but emptiness so far.

Come and step right into my life.
Oh come my lovely pumpkin, come.
The wheels of time rendered me rife,
My spirit has been too lonesome.

The crowd around me just ignores
My silent cries all through the years.
They repeat encore and encore
That I fake the roots of my fear.

But suddenly, as summer rain,
You watered down my lonely drought.
It took no sweat, it took no pain
But you answered my silent shouts.

So come my little God sent, come,
Come take what you solely deserve.
Come be the dawn of my night, come,
Come take what is for you reserved.

Faith Versus Reason

When you roam over me, daring and audacious,
Fearlessly insulting my theme in every way,
Shadowing all my thoughts, raging loud, tell me, say,
Do you gleam in essence, make me more fallacious?

You challenge all my words, scoffing vociferous,
But Lo! I come strewing and still for you I pray.
Parried and defeated, many threats you display
But in vain. For in spite, I remain victorious.

I draw my humble strength from divine providence
Unveiled to you only if you join in my stance
And bow down free of pride and patiently loving.

Only then will He show to you boundless treasures
Drawn from the bleeding Heart, from the Word-flesh living,
Maker of all the stars, Source of divine pleasures.

Feeling Down

Oh how dreadful it seems
The time spent all alone,
Just like in scary dreams
The time drags on and on.

You use all resources
From your spiritual safe,
Often open sources
To feed into your faith.

You call on your Father
Who always delivers
Hoping He will offer
Help to one who suffers.

But you are so distraught
That you cannot connect
And your disgruntled thoughts
Your prayer, do affect.

So you lie all weary
Awaiting the power
From the Lord Almighty
To brighten your hour.

And until He replies,
Gives you His grace anew
You cry and you despise
This aversion in you.

But be strong, you Christians,
Chosen of the dear Lord;
This rewards has demands
And price you can afford.

Never has it been said
That the heavy laden
Has been left unaided
Or had scorned his demand.

Flip of a Coin

(Sadly so)

Just like rushing against a
Transparent wall
And smashing your whole being
And in reverse fall
Is the feeling you get when a
Brethren you love but,
To your sad surprise, it is not reciprocated…

How sad it must have been
For you O my Lord Jesus!
How even more grievous
To know that unto You this is constantly perpetrated…
If one day His Voice you hear,
Harden not you heart if fear.

From Me to You

When it becomes all clear,
When the smoke is all gone
You will notice how near
You'll be to my person.

Just like me you waited
To reach this oasis,
This break long expected
Rendered your heart novice.

But you kept on your ground
And stuck to your standard,
When no solace you found,
Your hope, did not discard.

Then came that blessed eve
That saw your dream come true;
What you lost was retrieved,
In bundle sent to you.

Since now it is all clear
And your heart is renewed,
I can face all my fears
And declare I love you.

Fruit of Patience

No one will ever understand
The love that exists between us.
It will remain not obvious
Till our blessed time's at hand.

Happy are those who peacefully
Await the dawning of their day.
They always reap the precious whey,
The one they deserve rightfully.

For the patience they invested
Never fails in time to repay,
At their door all stumble one day,
At their door, where they were tested.

The love you make stem from my chest
Emerges from your tone of voice.
It narrows my array of choice
But keeps me hoping for the best.

So don't ask the world to fathom
The storm or reason of my thrill.
For never, never will they feel
The bliss that my world has become.

Grow Old

If ever I grow old,
Old, gray, weary and cold,
If ever I grow old,
In my heart, be it gold.

If ever I grow old,
Old so that I am told,
Fed, bathed even controlled,
Be my pride not too bold.

If ever I grow old,
Old with body of mold,
Let then love grab a hold
And gently rock my soul.

Happy Mother's Day

Happy Mother's day to you,
God rested when He made you
Then allowed, in His wisdom
That my way one day you'd come.

You're the loveliest lady
That this side of Albany,
With its unruly weather,
Could one day nurture ever.

Since the Lord provides the rest,
I wish you the very best
And hope that on Mother's day,
His divine Love comes your way.

Heartfelt Advice

So carry your burden, one minute at a time.
Carry your load of pain till the end of your day.
Soon tomorrow will shine and deliver your prime
For the Lord of goodness watches over your way.

On this journey called life, you meet friends, you meet foes.
This desert you're crossing will always be made of
Oasis and mirage cause of your highs and lows.
To what may come your way offer nothing but love.

Carry then your burden for the Spirit in you
Will guide your every step, give you strength and wisdom.
Since in all of your trails, thus far He's seen you through,
Remain ever faithful for better days will come.

Human Nature

The happiness we hunger for
Repeatedly nudges our sides,
Ever calling the mind ashore
Of the isles reality hides.

It's always such a bad sighting
To grasp the cold matter of fact
That human beings live for searching
Even when they have what they lacked.

Never we settle for a catch,
Never will we be satisfied,
Never will we secure the latch
Of craving for the other side.

Happiness will therefore remains
A star way up in the night sky.
It leads us through vales and mountains
Till at the end our spirits fly.

If You Were Mine

If you were mine, if you were mine
God knows how much I'd be happy,
Nor just ok, neither just fine;
You'd expel all my misery.

If you were mine, if you were mine,
I'd smile for the whole world to see.
No one for whom to yearn and pine,
I'd be singing in harmony.

The rain, the snow, the hurricane,
All swings of Mother Nature's mood,
Since on cloud nine, though in no plane,
Could never get my heart to brood.

Every morning I'd watch you rise
And immerse my self in your shine
Then daily gazing in your eyes,
I'd kiss your face if you were mine.

People

People come and people go,
Often it's a one-man show.
The one by your side today
Can always just fade away.

People come and people go
In your life like an arrow
Leaving in the aftermath
You, with heart of sociopath.

People come and people go;
Feels at time like a low blow
To grasp the cold-hearted fact
Numbing you like an infarct.

People come and people go
Worming their way in sorrow
When they're made to realize
They've been played before their eyes.

People come and people go
Then you're back to ground zero.
All the years you've invested
Leave your mouth bitter tasted.

People come and people go
Often leaving deep sorrow;
The air they displace with them
Leaves you stifling just the same.

People come and people go
That is as far as I know.
But then after they retreat
Study the message that's fit.

Since my sunshine has returned
And made all things so brand new,
I promise in fair return
To sunbathe and treasure you.

People come and people go
Making life dull and hollow
But thank God for destiny,
It's time for you my Junie.

And just like the breeze that blows
Bringing sunshine, bringing snow,
For as long as it echoes,
People will come and will go.

Pineyes

Only for the look of your eyes
I will dare the soundest reasons.
They are to me the sweetest prize
To cherish all through the seasons.

Their gentle glow that can appease
The concerns emerging in me,
Can easily, when you so please,
Provoke in my heart a love plea.

They shine their light in gloomy days,
Dry up the dew of misery,
They bridge a rainbow that relays
My dark cell to my reverie.

From afar they were the lighthouse
Guiding my raft unto your soul.
From afar I retained no doubts
That you would come and make me whole.

So for the look of those, your eyes,
I will face the fiercest of storms.
You're the genie that's fit to size
For my life much needed reforms.

Puzzled

I will never grasp how dry and shallow
The thoughts we whisper can be
If they are not from hence cannot echo
The divine Spirit Mercy.

With all the savez of these passing times
Grounded the heart should remain,
Deep within the Source of non-ending primes
That this life issues explain.

So blind and bitter the people remain
Whose insight is so shaded
By the glittering, the ever so vain
Point of view that now's faded.

The signs are galore, the calls ever strong
To be each other's keeper
For we have always come from thus belong
To the very same Father.

Refrain

The spring of life shapes up the road
Upon which you carry your load,
Heavy, whenever comes the fall,
Deprived of any fun at all.

You strive so hard to make amend
Too much laden and so saddened
And daily you are reminded
That all hopes have slowly faded.

And yet daily down on your knees
You promise, your Maker to please,
Although the heft of humanhood
Pressingly begs for carnal food.

But if you still mean to serve Him
Fill up your patience to the rim.
Nothing will bring a better smile
Than love spread all across your miles.

Always according to the code,
Always before your great download,
Always the goodness sown around,
Always to its source becomes bound.

Rose Shower…Shower of Love

It's raining roses from the blue sky
It's raining, what a delight!
It's raining, ecstasy
It's raining, we're happy
It's raining, the heart sings
It's raining happiness
It's raining, love carries us away
It's raining sea of roses
It's raining sweetness
It's raining tenderness
It's raining younger years,
Lasting years
It's raining loveliness
It's raining the heart cheers,
What a joy!
It's raining, we're kissing
It's thrilling
Hearts shivering
It's raining, sweet pleasure
Sheer rapture
Endless measure

It's raining, love brand new
Sweet as honey dew
Tearless years
Dawning years
Charming breeze
That hearts seize
At the sight
Of love's delight
It's raining from above
It's raining endless love…

But tomorrow
On us below
Love will bestow
Only sorrow
No more roses
Are falling
It's raining; lack of your presence
It's raining; perturbed quiescence
It's raining; boring rain
Causing pain
It's raining sad goodbyes
From the skies,
Non ending
Tears bringing

It's raining no more flowers
Only hours
Hoping
Longing
Moping
It's raining no more delight
Only fright
It's raining but…

For now on
Us upon
Only will pour
Sadness galore.
For now on
Tasteless feeling
For now on
Senseless living.
For the soul
Unmade whole
Withering
Like falling
Autumn leaves
Shallow breathe
In the mire
And expire.

Jhonnie and Wen

They came bearers of hidden gifts,
One not rested yet from her shift,
The other proudly displaying
The best sample of her siblings.

But yet they came, a lovely pair,
To mabuhay me square and fair.
We sat and chit chat over lunch
Taken in a bit of a rush.

And so they came while from my mind
My free speech I could hardly find.
It's not often that in one day,
So much affection comes your way.

So in return I wrote these lines
Quickly before the Eastern shines
Just to give a salamat po
To my cutest Cebu duo

Take Over

My state of mind is in peril,
It suffered a coup to its state.
A coup d'état as it stood still,
A coup d'état to seal its fate.

My state of mind's no more a state.
It now has become a province,
A province annexed to your fate,
Your fate that now has my last chance.

My state of mind therefore will be
A mere image of your caprice.
Wherever you travel you'll see
All sites branded by you I miss.

Painful

Down on my knees I come to You,
Ridded of pride, revived anew.
The tears burning my trembling cheeks
Surge from my soul all tame and meek.

Who would have thought that yesterday
So tall and proud, so vain and gay,
The abc's I so ignored
Would swing on me as an encore...?

Just Because It's Fall

I know just what you like, I know what you abhor.
I know what makes you sad and what you will fight for.
I know what tickles you, how much you love the fall,
And I know that's the time when I'll receive your call.

It's the best of seasons, when the sun always seems
To send to us its strong but rendered mellow beams.
It will shine then that day as to not to molest
You on the path you'll take, on the way to your nest.

You will return to me and Nature will approve.
The cushion of the leaves even your steps will soothe.
And the trees disrobing their precious apparel
Will tell you to restart, with no fuss, with no bell.

No wonder we name it the season of advent;
It's the time to prepare for most precious events,
Like the birth of a Child, the rebirth of Nature,
And the recovering of lost precious treasures.

So you'll return to me in the midst of the fall,
Your favorite season, I faithfully recall.
Because I know you well, oh yes, this I can tell,
You will reclaim your boo, with no fuss, with no bell.

Knight's Sight

And from within the night
Rendered cold by the fright,
Deep from within the night
You set on me your sight.

And all of a sudden
As in a fairy tale,
But in such a sudden
I became much less pale.

So then you took my hand,
Got me up on my feet.
I held on to your hand,
Afraid to leave my seat.

But you smiled tenderly,
Honest and loving soul,
Then giggled merrily
But did not dare lose hold

Of my poor lonely heart
Longing for a soul mate,
That one heart set apart
That'd come and change its fate…

But from within my night,
Despite my dreaded fright
You came and set things right
Once on me you set sight.

Last Breath

Even the last breath I exhale
Will be meant to call on your name.
It will emerge fragile and pale,
Bearing your colors just the same.

The life you live seeking a hand,
Seeking a hand firmly to hold,
Appears to you empty and bland
When you're feeling weary and cold.

So for the last time I will look
On my screen, my life flashing by,
Painfully mourning that it took
This tragedy for you to try

To grace my room with your presence,
And finally offer your hand,
This hand I sought as a last chance,
Just when my chance comes to an end.

So my last breath I will exhale
Peacefully calling out your name
Just to summarize the sad tale
Of a life spent seeking one's flame.

Laughter And Tears

The love I have for you to the world I confess,
The love that I treasure more than any richness,
The love I would offer on my knees like a pearl
To you my lovely child, till the end of the world.

With tears and with laughter we are educated.
Were not love in our hearts we would be ill fated.
So laugh my lovely child, your loving soul express,
With tears, down on my knees I love you, I confess.

Love Games

She was a friend, she said
Invited me, we played.
We had our game
Did not feel shame
Although the same
Others would blame.
Deep in her eyes
I saw disguise
And compromise.
But we held hands,
Hers was so cold.
The five year old
Feeling we hold
Remained as bold.
Love never ends.

Lovely

Lovely, you're so lovely,
As lovely as a rose.
Lovelier than the blue sky
After a summer rain,
Lovely as the Heavens
With a clear rainbow tie.
Lovelier than a starry night,
A humming bird in its still flight.
Lovely, but so lovely,
Lovely under the rain.
Lovely as a strong need
You're just about to feed.
As lovely as the sheets
Of lovers in retreat,
As lovely as the night
Caught by the dawn's first light.
As lovely as a child
In all his innocence,
As lovely as our love
Given this blessed chance,
As lovely as the eve
Of your first Christmas day,
As lovely and as fine
As the day you'll be mine.

Lovely, lovelier than before,
As lovely as the sun rising,
Lovely as though tribulating
You would've come out lovelier.
Lovely, so full of loveliness,
All emanating from your chest.
You seem to be so damn lovely
That I stand watching stunningly.
As lovely as the break of dawn
On a dejected spirit's lawn.
So you'll remain just as lovely
From the dawn till the end of day
You the one and you the only
Bringer of bright smiles and sunrays.

As would say Ricardo Arjona

Loving You

(Amarte a ti)

Loving you is not the best, this I know for sure,
Having so many things to do less traumatizing,
Like finding faces in the clouds,
Like going to the movies or doing nothing.

Loving you is not the best but I like it.
Maybe I'm playing as always at being masochist,
Instead of entertaining myself with soccer
Or with the Internet like every one does.

Loving you is not the best but it's perfect
For it give some sense to this routine
Of being always only a citizen, only just that.

Loving you makes me suffer, but I am so fortunate.
For it reminds me that I exist and that I feel,
For it gives me something to think about all night long, makes me alive.

Loving you is venom that gives life.
It's a torch that brightens up when turned off.
It's the sublime coupling the nonsense,
It's a feeling; therefore who'd understand?

Loving you is the most fabricated truth.
It's the best of the worst I've ever experienced.
It's Russian roulette for a kiss,
It's just so unpredictable.

Loving you is an error, a friend told me.
He believes that being happy is being free
But fails to understand the thrill of the unknown.

Loving you is a flickering moment in my mind,
It's also having hated you now and then,
Loving you is just absurd and we both know it
But it'll stay this way…as long as it lasts.

Main Squeeze

I will not attempt to tell you
The load of thoughts submerging me.
I won't even hint to your view
The lines my queries carved deeply

On my forehead trying to hide,
To keep the world free of worries,
The pressing matters deep inside,
The ones fueling my dream series…

The part of me you've always been,
That part my other part treasures,
The part I'd seek through thick and thin,
That part source of all my pleasures.

That part in me I keep alive,
That part leads me in all I do.
For all I do in this here life
Shows the love I partake with you.

I will therefore keep well concealed
The many words I could tell you
For they carry sadness and thrill
Depending on your psyche too.

You will always know what I feel,
You will always dictate my mood,
You will always come and reveal
To my mind when it's time to brood.

Meet Me at BJ's

Turn left in the aisle, step into my heart,
With your blank affect and your BJ's cart.
I needed someone to feel my poor half,
It just so happened that you crossed my path.

I always wanted to be close to you
But just out of sync we were through and through.
So when I saw you on that clear fall day,
I rightly took it; you were sent my way.

Lovely you have been, lovely you remained.
Even all the wakes never could refrain
You from blooming cute, cute as a button,
Beautiful Vicky dreamed of for so long.

So now that you turned around my corner,
The lonesome corner of my poor ticker,
Step right in my love, make yourself at home,
We waited too long; let's write our own tome.

Mighty Deeds

And for a long, long time
We waited for this time.
Time of peace, time of joy,
Free of the least alloy.
Time that will make us see
That among the many
Who came seeking a break
We too had what it takes
To make it yet so far
While many lost their star.

For long, long time ago,
Searching high, searching low,
We always came up short
Of peace of any sort.
So we went on faking
To all the human beings
While what we had inside
Was nothing else but pride
And the whole reason why
Peace to us was so shy.

But now we understand,
It's been so well explained,
That what you so receive
And that so often grieves
Is drawn from the many
Actions that we carry.
So always keep in mind
That you ought to be kind
For your deeds have power
To bring tears or laughter.

My Muse

When I sit alone with my thoughts,
When I empty my daily load,
When from all the goals that I sought,
The ones that popped up on my road,

My mind sizzles in hot debate,
When I go search down my alleys
The reasons crushing down my fate
But come with nothing but follies,

When finally I can affront
My old pucker in the mirror
Knowing that all the dos and don'ts
Were handled with tact and honor,

When the concerns this world offers,
The ones I ponder all day through,
Seem to overtake the laughter
Charging our stamina anew,

Then you surface with all your charm,
Quintessence of all reveries,
Bringing to my soul in alarm
A sucker to ease my worries…

Always then when I sit alone
Of my concerns I'm not afraid
Knowing that once you're on your throne
My petty thoughts and cares just fade.

My Chérie

I have me a little baby
Really sweet as sweetness can be.
I have me a little chérie
Chasing away my misery.

She came and poured out all her care,
Venturing where none tried to dare.
When all before failed miserably,
She came lighthearted and bubbly.

She instilled love a brand new way.
She always has nice things to say.
She cracks you up day after day
And fills you with joy come what may.

In return she simply demands
That her efforts you understand
And that you carry with both hands
Her candid heart upon your stand.

I have me a little baby
With love as strong as one can be.
I have me a little chérie
That very soon I will marry.

My Darling

Just wanted to tell you how sweet your embrace feels
And how holding you near marvels me to the chills.
The magic of the bay, the still peace of your room
Made that last Sunday night ecstatic, free of gloom.

I had to be away from what I so treasure
To swear not to ever refrain from such pleasure.
You made me feel so new, so warm and so alive
That I declare aloud that you're my better halve.

I love you my darling and for so strong reasons
That I often wonder why do I stay alone.
But to rush is to fail. Nothing is finalized
Unless it is over and over analyzed.

So darling we'll get there though again we may face
Either tougher rival or even bigger mace.
Enough, I said enough, let me just end my rhyme
With the sweet taste I have of getting back my prime.

My Future Wife

You must be somewhere waking up
Or this day about to wrap up.
Your parents around you may be
Caring for your every hobby.

Or is it that alone like me,
You're moping in your misery?
Are you somewhere soaking the sun
Or in a place where rays there' none?

Does it matter? Not so ever.
For you, my heart in its whispers,
Rehearses over and over
The words of love that it harbors.

We'll meet one day or have we yet
Exchanged words that we did forget?
Does it matter, does it ever?
Love's always been a pathfinder.

My Infused Love

I come humbly to let you know
How my whole life belongs to you.
All through my highs, all through my lows,
Despite my fog, your light shines through.

I come humbly when time's at hand
To pour my whole self at you feet.
All that I made, all that I planned
Breathe your body, mind and spirit.

I come humbly and don't pretend
To be the one sharing your dreams.
But rather I want to attend
At the least of your silent screams.

So on my knees I come humbly
Daily to count you my worries.
Funny how jovial and bubbly
My spirit flips in a hurry.

For to your almost divine grace
I'll always bring my weary soul
And to you and your lovely face
Forever give my heart to hold.

And naturally when times are rough
And my spirit travels wobbly,
When all dopey I reach my trough,
Again to you I'll come humbly.

My Karen

So lovely is my Karen,
So poised when she does her thing,
That with her air of Greek goddess
She bathes her world with easiness,

So quiet is my Karen,
So tranquil and so pleasing,
That with her stare vaguely eerie
She'll make a foe of a chéri.

So frisky is my Karen,
So lively yet all bearing,
That with the grace of her presence
You feel you'll get another chance.

But Karen is the one queen
Whose kingdom though fair and keen
Would never open up its gate
And change of my heart the debate.

My Marijune

To the heck of the girl I love,
The one I can't get enough of,
I want to send this written kiss
Just so she knows how much she's missed.

I quiver, quiver all inside,
Though many times I tried to hide
The effect her lovely brown eyes
Provoke in me they hypnotize.

My hands are still seeking the touch
Of her hands, her skin and so much.
Always she's the one to instill
Within my soul her warmth so real.

So to this little girl I love,
This precious, petable, sweet dove
I offer a whole world of these,
Kisses and hugs…what a délice!

Winter Morn

On such a gray morning,
Rainy, cold, dark and still,
On such dreary morning
My soul I yearn to fill.

The gray sky to the trees
Seems to become good friend
And with conniving ease
The bright sun they curtain.

Not a sound, not a bird,
Not even a squirrel,
No engine to be heard
That would the day herald.

Life itself seems to hang
In this tenacious mist.
But the dawn that long rang,
The night cannot resist.

And the day crushed under
This penetrating fog
Seems to miss the wonder
Of a warm sunshine hug.

So we all miss the sun
And its beautiful rays
While my soul thirsts for none
But my Bread of today's.

Then to You, my Master,
I open my spirit.
Touch it divine Healer,
Fill it with loving treats.

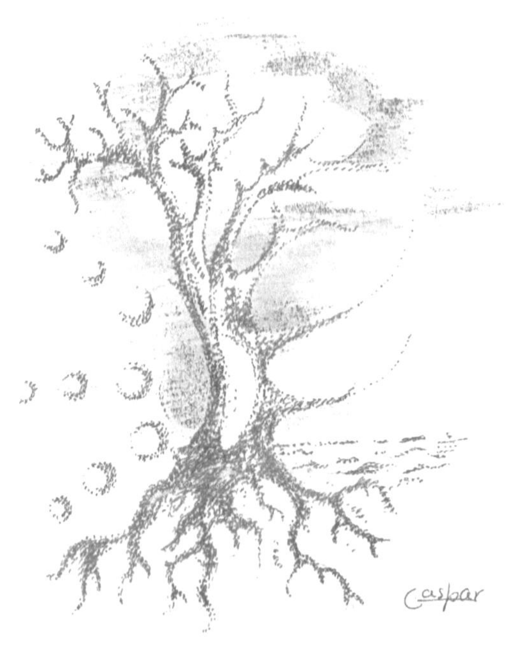

When my Junie was Mine

I don't know why I try to write thoughts of this kind.
Maybe cause day and night they occupy my mind
Or maybe just because the mere fact of writing
Open large avenues for deeper soul searching.

Every time I awake my faithful memory,
I marvel at the point I reach; sad and teary.
It brings about a flow of strong and gushing blood,
It brings about the time when on my turf she trod.

Yes when Junie was mine I never had a clue,
Looking at that young girl, that my dream had come true.
I gambled night and day, betting on her strong love,
Disregarding the signs, sheer warnings from above.

Each time I went away I could not fathom why
That sense of doom I felt would bring me heavy sighs.
But the fool that I was never saw the cold tomb
Awaiting my poor self, lined up with finest gloom.

So when Junie was mine slowly I let her go,
So much desiring to restart from zero.
But little did I know that when she left the nest
My cold and stifling soul followed the very best.

My Promise

One day if the good Lord allows,
One day of fall, to say the least,
One day I'll gladly take my vows,
One day I'll do what I promised.

The morning rain would have just stopped,
The sun would then shine a bit pale,
The birds from their nests would come pop;
They'd all rush to witness the tale.

Nature tends, in a lot of ways,
To prepare special happenings.
Even the earth won't speed away
From the bliss this good day will bring.

One day therefore, of clear blue sky,
One day, strolling along the pier,
With witnesses, the passers-by,
I'll entrust to you my life, dear.

My Pursuit of Happiness

From the day I was born,
That January morning,
At my first sightseeing
I saw your lovely horns.

You came to visit me
In the arms of your Mum.
But sucking on your thumb,
You put your stamp on me.

Never knew what hit me
But ever since that day
Every time that we play
My day became merry.

We grew up steadily,
I, a dorky young man,
You, a lovely maiden
Who became a lady,

And the many princes
Who came after your hand,
They made me understand
That I'd lost all chances

I had to be happy
Or display just the same
While so trying to tame
My deep, silent fury.

But when you left the turf,
Left me sad, left me cold.
Left me nothing to hold
But my young age to surf.

I had my ups and downs,
Made my share of mistakes,
Collected my heartbreaks
And in turn made some frown.

When again I saw you
You had time to marry.
I listened silently
To your every booboo.

So many you sustained.
They came so steadily
But changed not how jolie
A queen you had remained.

I tried to wave at you,
Timidly, cautiously,
Aware wholeheartedly
Of what I had to do.

With my heart on my sleeve
I came to your abode,
Tried in vain to download
To you my love missives.

You would not take the bait,
You would not consider.
You had picked another
Who again scarred your fate.

That's when I left the state
Hoping for some fresh air,
Found her fair, found her square
But she was born too late.

So I came back anew,
Was placed right in your midst.
Since I could not resist,
I stayed away from you.

Life with us plays its game
And one can never tell.
One evening, with no bell,
To your sighting I came.

Around you time stood still,
Around you nothing lived.
I tried hard to reprieve
This gush of blood so real.

But what came loud and plain
Was the verbiage in me,
This flow strong and steady,
This stifled love refrain.

Until my life expires,
Until I breathe no more,
Until on other shore
You'll be my soul's desire.

I long for your embrace,
I long to be with you.
I long to be renewed
By the smile of your face.

This is my poor appeal;
To reach out and connect.
Don't shun the shy effect;
It's deep the love I feel.

Again I come to you,
Again, just to reveal
That for your squeeze I will
Long for my whole life through.

I'll always pursue you,
My source of happiness.
You have been my mistress
Long, long before you knew.

My Swallow

My swallow has landed
Despite her broken wings.
She flew but went stranded,
Laden with sufferings.

My swallow has landed,
She dropped down in her nest.
She came empty handed
But with love in her chest.

My swallow has landed
Despite her many tears.
Her heart of love loaded
Made it easy to steer.

And so with arms opened,
Ready to love I stand
For now until the end
My swallow is on land.

My True Love

The inspiration arising
From deep within the hushed up soul
Comes all stamped up, loudly crying,
Unveiling to us stirring tolls.

There, in the midst of black and white
We read clearly the promises
So unspoken and out of sight
Though their words bear hugs and kisses.

It's always an opened window
Of lonely cage left in the cold.
From it will escape a swallow,
First sign of what is yet untold.

So when my pen speeds unafraid,
Revealing thoughts branded by you,
With no scheme, ponder what is said;
I brag of you, my love so true.

My Words

Sometimes the words that I shower
Your ears, as a passionate kiss,
Are never robed in the power
I try to share with you I miss.

They remain lame, they remain weak,
They fail miserably too much.
They don't carry the warmth I seek,
To melt you heart with hugs and such.

But repeatedly they emerge
Trying to bring my loving stamp
And more than often what they surge
Is an image all pale and damp.

But they come back with the intent
To reach their goal next time around.
And they won't feel any content
Until from them pure love abound.

And so my words relentlessly
Will come caress your lovely ears
Till they dislodge successfully
From within you all trace of fear.

Night Reply

In the still of the night
All is calm, not so bright.
We can hear the long sighs
Echoing all the lies
Brought from every living
Creature earth is stirring.

In the still of the night
All the wrongs appear right.
Or so it has to be
Or else we'd never see
What really could have been
Had it all come so keen:

…Often the many doors for us made wide open.
The silent knight escorts that by our side remain…

But then we see the moon
And think it came too soon,
Still we never perceive
The yet simple missives
That every time night falls
The weakened mind recalls.

Hope for a brand new day
To always come your way.
Have faith in all your dreams
Despite what they may seem.
They are though they look dim
Answers to silent screams.

GOD's Love

The time we spend searching for love
Should be spent with the God above
For only He knows well our hearts.

He provides for all our needs
And He daily our spirits feeds
For He made us all from the start.

He came on earth to spread His Love,
The love we are so in need of,
The one that makes us wise and smart.

For only by sharing His love
In return we get from above
The fondest desires of our hearts

Ode to my Junie

Never will you unfold this puzzling mystery
That daily I sustain deep in my heart and mind,
Never, I say never, do not waste your query;
The cause remains hidden, not for the world to find.

The mighty waves of sea cover lesser treasure,
Even the universe offers no such richness.
And the immense azure so blue in its rapture
Still retells but poorly the charms of my mistress.

From the dawn of the day till the sun retires,
From the East to the West, even between the Poles,
From the driest of sands, right where the sun fires
To the greenest pasture with merry bunny holes,

Nothing offers a sound warmer in decibels,
Nothing can bring a tune with better harmony,
Nothing, I say nothing; the universe babbles
When it nears the warm voice of my lovely Junie.

On my Mind

The thoughts of you that linger on
Give me rainbow to glide upon.
They mastermind a safe heaven
Where I retire quite often.

There, all my dreams of me and you
Never leave my elated view.
They free my soul of all bondage
And to my heart they give courage.

Never knowing a dull moment,
Always giving me great content.
They can, if given direction,
Cause a spectrum of emotions.

For if ever you were to shun
My plea for some rays of your sun,
These thoughts of bliss and revelry
Would turn to hell and misery.

For my world's so wrapped around you;
It can be bright, it can be blue.
It can be built or fall apart
All based on the mood of your heart.

So when you come and nudge my soul
Keep in mind that you take control
Of this fellow so far away
Who bear your thoughts in bare display.

Up in the Air

Up in the air
There is no dimension,
A sense of slow motion,
For way up there
Regardless of poundage
You feel out of a cage.

It's only fair
That for His creation
God has this equation;
That in the air,
Regardless of your age,
You sleep or turn a page.

One Person

One person in my life it seems,
One person to fulfill my dreams.
One person with a lovely smile,
One person I've known for a while.
One person to make my sun shine,
One person who would claim she's mine.

One person in my arms to dwell,
One person, I know, I can tell.
One person I've been dreaming of,
One person I so long to love.
One person whom my heart beats for,
One person to settle my score.

One person to wrap in my arms,
All dazzled by her childish charms,
One person to say I love you,
One person to pet all life through.
One person I'd give stars and moon,
To one person, my Marijune.

Outraged

The phone rings, you answer.
I greet you, the winner.
Seems you've won the battle.
"I can stand the tackle",
I once thought in my mind.
But you were not so kind
When you bet I would come
Beg you cause I'm lonesome.

But the game that you play, cold and egocentric,
Exposes to the world the you narcissistic.
And the many victims in your luscious web caught
Graduate Cum Laudae; in your school they were taught.

They leave brokenhearted but rich in experience,
They learn to distinguish rare pearl from cheap brilliance.
But just in case your mind still ponders the reason
My voice today you hear, I tell you, there is none...

I would not look at it this way if I were you,
In the state I am now, any old dog would do.

Shackled

(Love triangle)

At night when I wonder what became of your smile,
When the only echo is my frantic heartbeat,
When I fight with the thought that even for a while
He would come next to you rightfully take his seat,

I become well aware of this senseless posture
I slowly slid into, though I fought it so well.
Riveted by your charm, docile in your capture,
My soul became ablaze; but this no one could tell.

Who would in my lifetime have revealed to me such?
Who would in their right mind have come up with this score?
Who would have dared foretell this agonizing crush
Tearing me in pieces, unlike ever before?

No, never will I drown into this sea of pain,
Never will I allow my heart to bleed anew.
Patience is a virtue that only the wise gains
Through daily dose of love, against all odds in queue.

At night when I wonder, I pause then for a while.
For though I hear echo of my frantic heartbeat
And I fight with my thoughts, my love not to defile,
I refrain, mind and soul, from declaring defeat.

Silent Words

Should I tell you how much I love you?
How you have made my dream come true?
The silent words I don't utter
Deep inside of me I mutter.

You should not hear the strong racing,
You should not see the blank staring,
You should ignore that through my day
Nothing, nothing comes in your way.

You take over at early dawn
And often comes to trip my yawn
For the smile surging within me
Carries your stamp, O my baby.

So there, these words I don't utter
Always come causing my laughter.
Along with you, my dream came true,
So why should I say I love you?

So Sorry

And for the life of me I thought that I loved you.
Always thought that with you all my dreams would be true
I had plans for a life tailor-made for us two
Hidden in the safe of my heart.

I for a long, long time imagined future days
Filled with love and laughter warmed up by the sunrays
And with warm starry nights that'd fill the month of May;
Display of divine work of art.

Those dreams I almost lived, so vivid in my mind,
Provoked for the most part by your loving so kind,
Were always within me, almost making me blind
To the real motives that you had.

But it was all so nice, so brand new and so strong
That from the very start I thought that I belonged
By your side and nothing between us could go wrong;
But to you it was just a fad.

So there it was one day into my life you came
But without any words you left me just the same
And I searched but in vain for someone else to blame;
I alone sealed my destiny.

So for now on empty-handed and pitiful
Around my world, a load of emptiness I pull,
Every sunrise makes it harder to keep my cool
So sorry I lost you honey.

Specially for You

I really suffer your pain,
I drown in your despair
Since we're spiritually one.
But since physically I am stronger
I'll do the spirit lifting.
Babe, regardless of what you're going under
Strong faith, you have to keep up.
It will have to be your last resort
When resort you run out of.

I've been for the past years praying for you.
Every time I go to my Lady of Czestochowa
I always pray for you, light candle in your name.
Have faith honey, have faith. I can talk about it all day long.
You will never comprehend
How primordial it is in the life of a Christian.
Believe babe, believe
And watch your Father do what He does best.

Speechless

The many words I cannot find
Come play in meadows of my mind
Heralding the reality
That you're now my eternity.

The many words I cannot find
Though unspoken, they fall behind
And watch my heart dragged on a leash
By your sweet name that I cherish.

The many words I cannot find
Will never see, they are too kind,
The calm effect that on my sea
Your words impress, O my chérie.

I sit and slowly take the thrill
That your love to my heart instills.
It's unique and disrupts always
My peace of mind, my end of days.

The many words I cannot find
When thoughts of you run through my mind
Pronounce what I long discovered
That I will be yours forever.

Suffering

Follows us like a shadow,
Always causing us sorrow,
In our hearts digs its burrow,
This is our suffering.

Many times we try to shy,
Often coming up with lies,
Shutting doors when it does pry,
This is our suffering.

Even when we cheat our way,
The truth, refuse to convey
Close to us it comes to stay,
This is our suffering.

Our standard we may change,
Our plans we may rearrange,
It always seeks its revenge,
This is our suffering

It seems to be a part of our basic nature.
Unlike wisdom, waits not that we fully mature.
It is a flagrant part of our existence
Scruples, doubts, anxieties will not give any chance
To the laden spirit.

All the saddened goodbyes of our beloved ones,
The crushing betrayals experienced more than once,
When death comes suddenly a dear one to retrieve,
When we want to forget but just cannot forgive,
The heart feels great deceit.

The third part of ourselves is never forgotten.
We don't need lots of years our pain to obtain.
We work hard all our life often until our death.
Sickness, worries and needs often perturb our health
And the body hauls it.

Time never stops in its scope
To deprive us of our hope.
We worry about the past,
Afraid of the debts it left.
The present time will not last
Still we experience its heft.
The future observes the scene
And makes us feel deep within
The weight of its doubts and frights
When we're faced with all its "might's".

Alone with this heavy weight
Fit to crush the meekest soul,
To carry on with this freight
Faith is all humans should haul.

For only by offering
To the Lord our suffering
Will He give us peace within
And relief to our soul, bring.

Sweet Complaints

How painful is my loneliness
If you're not here smiling at me!
But what a thrill of happiness,
When you're around I feel so free.

The sea breeze is a mockery
When along I don't feel your breath.
But how sweet a feeling it'd be
If of your love I'd feel the depths.

The blue sky does not mean a thing,
It seems to size my affliction.
When we admire it I sing
And conceal no more dejection.

Even the twilight I cherish
Looks so dreadful. But of your eyes
The twinkle seems to embellish
And change all into paradise.

"Thanksgiving"

"Do you say the same prayer
Every time before dinner?"
Was thrown at me suddenly.
So I pondered naturally:
Was she simply wondering
Or my rite, belittling?
I decided not to judge.

Having no time to answer,
A few minutes don't linger,
That's all I had for dinner
Then to work return after.
The reply I thought since then
Within my heart, short and plain,
Remained solid as a grudge.

The blessings the Lord bestows,
Sometimes joy, sometimes sorrow,
Reveal the Father wisdom
Drawing us to His Kingdom.
His children should acknowledge
And not take this privilege
For granted; life is a trudge.

Often what we have today
That we are so sure will stay;
Good health, a job, a loved one,
Potential needs for someone,
May someday be swept away
So in gratitude we pray.
This way His Spirit, we nudge.

The Exit Door

We come into this world willfully, joyfully,
Cradled into the arms of well-chosen guardians.
We grow continuously, learning so steadily,
Until we reach the point of ultimate radiance.
We work, we procreate and we, in turn cradle
The ones who knowingly chose to call us parents.
We give off of ourselves, holding back a little,
Just enough to achieve the goal picked in advance,
Just waiting to become what we were once before.

And we share our treasures, the talents once given,
We carry each other, teach them what we were taught
We receive cheerfully whatever so often
Is offered in return; be it welcome or not.
Regardless how bitter a meeting may appear,
Either traumatizing, either ego scarring,
Maybe unexpected, or maybe longtime feared,
It remains in essence a source of stern teaching
Which if is overlooked comes back as an encore.

We live this life given the best we are able,
Sharing sorrow and pain, meeting friends, meeting foes,
Fighting with the ego, striving to stay humble
Despite the unfair deals, despite the many blows.
One after the other, despite what is suffered
One after the other we bring our input.
One after the other, we take what is offered
To help us tread alone while we remain en route
Hopefully, peacefully, towards the exit door.

The Deep Blues

And if I count the somber days
I spent chewing upon my thoughts,
Lonely, weary and all distraught
By the rubbish coming my way.

And if I reveal to my gents
The misfortune besetting me
And the resulting infamy
From these ever taunting events

Maybe at last they'll understand,
When ill-prepared for this journey,
The reasons why the so many
Take their destinies in their hands…

Let's not pretend to be appalled
By the thoughts these few lines contain.
Though you may fail to comprehend,
Deep blues to us all can befall.

The Last Day

The last day I saw you I can never forget.
We had said everything, we were ready and yet
There was this sense of doom, this feel of end of days,
This choking sensation of what I'll have to pay.

The last day I saw you, for some unknown reason,
I could perceive the price that would cost my treason.
But since I had to choose a trail way for my heart,
I opted painfully for my belle to depart.

The last day I saw you, was the last day I smiled.
The last day I saw you stayed with me a long while.
Repeatedly I dream of this crime to undo,
Repeatedly I dream instead, of choosing you.

The last day I saw you therefore I will retain,
I'll keep it till one day, atonement I obtain.
And hopefully, just as the balance I upset,
The purging of my soul this offense, will offset.

The Little Girl and the Doll

She stands alone talking sternly
To some father who's just sitting,
About his daughter whom frankly
He should care for above all things.

She rearranges furniture,
Cleans again the tiny tea set,
Giving her home a composure
For some guest not arrived as yet.

And now she pours the precious tea
Just to sample the sought flavor
Then asks the husband to go see
If it's those who came to savor.

The new recipe was worked at
Just when the baby took her nap.
But now she's crying like a brat
And nothing can get her to stop.

So she takes her back in her arms
Trying to walk her back to sleep.
Her face of five year old disarms
Anyone who would her watch keep.

And now school is just where it's at,
School is the corner of that chair,
That chair, cozy throne of the cat
Who jumps off thinking it's not fair,

Why should it be the one troubled,
Why can't she play in the lobby,
Why bother me, it thinks, muddled,
Frightened by this frozen baby…

The storybook she holds open
Is read aloud but upside down
And the student is asked often
To say words unknown to this town.

And just amid the words she goes,
Prompted by a Gap commercial,
Back to the house to change her clothes,
And dress her with the essential.

"And your father will be here soon
So you better do your homework,
Then you can go and watch cartoons,"
She told her with a childish smirk.

Then she swings her hair to the side
To mimic her mother's gesture
And carefully she goes to hide
The remote in her mother's fur.

And so the doll remains haggard,
With stare frozen of disbelief.
She would not dare give one regard
To her mother so stern and stiff.

Lucky for it: "Dinner is served,"
Says the mother from the next room.
The little girl has to reserve
Her fantasy in early bloom.

The New Chapter

And suddenly there was a knock.
It came out loud with no warning.
It stepped in without wavering
Despite all their doors double locked.

The tone of voice offered that night
Clearly rang out like Christmas bells.
Even deaf-mutes could surely tell
Of their message the subtle might.

So then and there the hook was placed,
Anchoring hearts mercilessly.
The talk went on too happily
With a much too déjà vu pace.

The homey feeling in the air
Ignored the thousand lengthy miles.
The tone of voice wearing big smiles
Was heralding a brand new pair.

If you could see the hold of hands
You'd feel the moisture of the palms.
Rather each milieu remained calm
Of the words to savor the strand.

But you could feel that time stood still,
Too much involved in this, its plot.
It felt that it waited a lot,
That this had to have the right feel.

So in the midst of the echo
Profoundly it planted the seeds.
One by one like rosary beads,
The long miles faded from the show.

The more of thoughts that were exchange,
The closer themes were then unveiled.
And all attempts just poorly failed
At quelling this joyful revenge

Of these two souls' jokes and laughter
From their bondage gladly set free.
And since the heavens heard their plea
They went to start a new chapter.

The Path

The path leading me to your door
Is lengthy as lengthy can be.
Its dreary and barren décor
Offers nothing for eyes to see.

The path leading me to your door
Is loaded with all kind of traps
Designed to trip me way before,
Of your treasure I find the map.

The path leading me to your door
Displays signs of alternative,
They bring me temptations galore
And ignore every nay I give.

The path leading me to your door
Appears to me so challenging.
It builds me stronger evermore
And to be with you so willing.

I will welcome this long journey,
Give up of the world the richness,
Even crawl down on my bare knees
To be with you my sweet princess.

The path leading me to your door
And its hurdles I will embrace,
Just to see the one I adore
And kiss and kiss her lovely face.

The Words I Say

It's always what I say; it's never what I write.
I see you so clearly, like the moon late at night,
Like the Bethlehem star on my lengthy journey,
You surely lead my heart to you, my sweet Junie.

It's always what I say though sometimes I recite:
"I can't fall out of love though she's so out of sight".
Just like the sure anchor of this boat in distress
Carefully I hang on to you, my sole mistress.

It's always what I say, fearing to feel the fright
Of rising tomorrow in darkness or in light.
The dusk that would befall if I never see you
Or the dawn I'll enjoy the day my dream comes true.

It's always what I say; say you will, say you might
Turn back the hands of time, come back and hold me tight.
And like nature's rebirth at the dawning of spring,
Over my cold season return and do your thing.

This Force

This Force given to me when I first saw the sun
Often makes that I look to the Heavens above,
Filled with melancholy, wishing I were a dove,
To my beautiful Source of loving bliss, return.

This Force is so mighty, prevents us from decay,
Teaches insidiously to choose from right or wrong.
It's the gift so precious we receive from day one
Making us wise and strong to meditate and pray.

For by praying alone this Force in us will grow.
Pray just to be grateful, we are so privileged
To be called His children; oh this is a sweet edge!
Pray with faith, pray alone, not just when in sorrow.

This Force in you and I gives us life, animates,
Helps us carry burden and with crosses it grows,
Makes us love another, waiting for life to close
Its doors when at the end with death we will have dates.

I dedicate my life to this one Force, nurture.
Regimen of prayers, good deeds, humility,
Hoping with His mercy to reach eternity,
That's all He asks of me, not fret for the future.

Thoughts…

I want to say so much
That I think you should know;
I love you…
I need you…
You're the sun of my night…
But in vain words I search
That could describe the glow
Around you,
Straight from you;
My thoughts put up a fight.

You'll never comprehend
How vulnerable I feel
With my heart in your hands
Making silent appeal
That you remain gentle,
Loving, kind and jolly,
Yet crazy a little
But not dilly-dally.

I caught myself worrying
Bout losing you one day;
Dreadful thoughts
Silly thoughts
That express of my heart
The depths of the feeling
From me coming your way;
Loving thoughts,
Merry thoughts
Wishing we never part.

To my Long Gone Buddy

(Yves-Benz Charles)

Often I think of you and the time we once had,
We were kids growing-up; our deeds were not so bad.
We climbed up steep mountains, explored hidden places,
Met people so often not seeing their faces.

Life took us overseas, we both our separate way.
We just could not prevent destiny and its sway.
We tried to keep in touch, started writing letters,
You stayed on the mainland, but I chose St Peter's.

Funny how so often my thoughts came over you,
Assuming that one day you would come back anew
And that it would be you and I as it was then
But lazy I remained and never took a pen.

At times I would recall that clear Sunday morning
You came down from Boston and left that same evening.
But little did I know that after that long drive
It would be the last time I would see you alive.

When I heard of the news that you had passed away
From that dreadful sickness… that was all they could say,
The pain I felt inside, still strong up to this day
Brings back to my blank mind your charm and funny ways.

Love

Love should be given hopelessly,
In return expecting nothing.
May what you spread generously
Not come back to you shortchanging!

The love you sow along your path
Blesses your divine counterparts.
In return the Giver of life
Grants the desires of your heart.

Foolish is the one who believes
That he should pamper himself first.
By serving others one retrieves
Graces galore that one can trust.

For the connection that we share,
Precious and divine in aspects,
Makes that minding others' welfare
Brings back a positive effect.

But this should not be the reason
We care for the needy brethren;
Love resides in every person
Then should be cherish and sustained.

I love you therefore hopelessly,
I love you with my heart and soul.
Cherish you I will do daily
Until we are a blessed whole.

Well, It's Valentine

Would I ignore this Valentine?
Could I wait for another year,
Fail to celebrate what is mine?
I was just teasing you, my dear.

Once a year this chance is offered
To express what lies in the chest,
Do you think I would have smothered
This new flame burning at its best?

There may not be another year,
People come and go all the time,
But since the time for us is here
I want to celebrate my prime.

So happy Valentine sweetheart,
May your day be warm and merry!
May the Lord, who keeps us apart,
Watch over your way, my chérie.

Your Eyes

When I look in your eyes I see my horizon.
So many times before I gazed in other skies
But like deer to water I come back to reason
And return faithfully to you, my lovely prize.

So many times before I have tried willingly
To leave their peaceful glow and lively tenderness
But always I return to your arms my jolie,
Happy to be your own, with loving eagerness.

They remain the mirror, in which I size my world,
They reflect the fervor of the love in your heart.
They are the loving cause my love for you unfurled.
They are now the reason we cannot stay apart.

Your eyes, my darling dear, remain my horizon.
More than enough I gazed into different skies.
But just like a swallow chasing better season,
Faithfully I come back, spellbound by your brown eyes.

Your Goodnights

It's always when you shut the door,
The door of your luscious palace
That left alone, confuse and poor,
I miss the fair glow of your face.

Never am I prepared for this;
I cling to you as breath of air.
Never. But each time you dismiss
This soul of mine I just can't dare

To face the world and its demands,
Its miseries and its failures.
In you only I can ascend
To what Heaven's for us creatures.

So I step right in this nightmare,
'Fraid of losing my sanity,
My sanity that I find where
Your voice in my ears ring, sweetie.

You shed your rain on my parade
Or spread rainbows on my downpour.
You are this sun that never fades,
This bliss I never knew before.

So when on me you shut the door
Of your place and you say goodnight
Despite promise of an encore
I still remain with heart of fright.

Your Voice

If I remain hushed up when you're talking to me,
If I drink every word you utter faithfully
It's because of your voice the melodious sound
Stirs bubbles in my heart, laughter in me abound.

It seems hard to describe what I internalize:
True beauty still remains in the beholder's eyes,
But your voice is lovely, your speech so full of zest,
Mostly when you go miles without taking a rest.

So talk my lovely bird, make music to my ears,
It can hold back the world but then it reappears
With noise of everyday and petty miseries
And pets that went away and dreadful maladies…

The greatest symphonies,
The wind in forest trees,
And the brook babbling down,
The swallow with no frown,
And the newborn gurgling
All, they don't mean a thing
When in me your voice rings.

Planely Dreaming

And all of the sudden,
As in a slow parade
Right from the window pane,
They linger by then fade.

You see gigantic fights
Frozen right on their tracks,
Monsters of shady white
With multi camel backs.

See this lovely lady
With a horse in her arms,
It is in no hurry
But slowly losing charms.

Then you seem to emerge
From a powder of air
In time to just submerge
A scene of love affair.

Often the things you see
With your bewildered eyes
Remain deep in the sea
Of your mind and surprise

Even you, beholder,
Who with no stimuli
Would never discover
Those, which in your mind lie.

Before you realize
The scenes the clouds excrete
From your brain mesmerized;
You land on the concrete.

Reaching Out

It always starts with no warming,
When the least I hear the calling.
It's a sudden, physical need
To sit and your charming voice heed.

But since I'm not in your circle,
The effect leaving me crippled,
Eludes the calm seen on your face,
But my frowning does not erase.

Right then I sit with my machine
And I spend, as in living scenes,
Dear moments between you and me
Long hours with you, my baby.

I can tell you so many things,
I can unveil all my feelings,
I can even hear the answer
And the smile I hear you offer.

Reaching out's always easy
When you dear visage I don't see.
Reaching out, holding your face,
While you give into my embrace.

Every morning is a good time
To tell you my love with my rhyme.
Every night comes as an encore;
I can kiss the face I adore.

Reaching out therefore I will do
Then email my poetry to you,
Until one day, out reaching,
Finally embrace the real thing.

Forever

Now that we've entered forever,
Now that we met at the crossroad,
Now that, at the age of silver,
For life we are blest to reload

On someone to ride the front seat,
On someone to worry about,
To share the joys and the defeats,
The seasons of rain and of drought.

Once again since we have the chance
To hold the taste of what's so dear,
To rekindle our dear romance
Against all the odds and the fears,

We can, since we are empowered,
Safeguard this recovered treasure.
We can, since we have been showered
With blessings beyond our measure.

We will therefore, at light of dawn
Give thanks for what we don't deserve.
And when the moon shines on the lawn
We will pray our love to preserve.

So many times in history
People given this chance once more,
Taking for granted His mercy,
Had lost what they so bargained for.

We paid a price of heavy toll
With long years of sorrow and pain.
We should avoid any dice roll
That'd jeopardize this love again.

So now that you are in my arms,
Now that I can hold you so tight.
Now that I, laden by your charms,
Will get to kiss you through the night,

I solemnly, to the Heavens,
Declare my overdue promise
To be yours until my life ends,
Cherish you till my heartbeats cease.

Be Still

No I won't be somber though my heart is aching,
I need my air to breathe, my most needed of things.
The emptiness around desolates, excruciates.
My soul down in the pits stifles without his mate...
Oh how I miss my baby!

No I won't be somber though 'round me there's dullness,
Even the simplest word from her would come caress
My spirit's broken wings, dragging his misery,
When the mind to the heart sends out no more query.
Oh how I love you, chérie!

I will drag all this load and go to my Father,
Humbly and silently my sorrow will offer.
He from whom all good things are sown in abundance
To my dejected soul will extend forbearance.
Oh Lord, show me mercy!

No I won't be somber though my life has no sense,
Though the smallest of grin seems to be an offense
To the thoughts I harbor, I will not be obscure.
Things are so much better that seem worst, I am sure...
Oh God, protect my honey!

Farewell

I will go on my separate way,
No more I love you will I say.
Since the string of love you sever',
There will be no more us, ever.

Repeatedly, time and again
You made it very, very plain,
That me, myself and all my love,
You wanted none of the above.

Once you uproot yourself, you said,
Made up your mind three years this may,
Nothing on earth would make you change,
Not ever your life rearrange.

So now the love table has turned;
To have your hand, I long and yearn,
Begging of you to please accept
The plea of love that I excerpt.

The knells of life did once again
Ring out to make me understand
That what you may find in the night
You lose sometimes in broad daylight.

At the Table

You sit again at the table
And not a thought springs from your mind.
You know you're willing and able
But you can't write what you don't find.

You're so willing to come connect
The many words found at your reach
But the combo you may select
Seems not to do what they so preach.

So you're faced up with a senseless
Pile of words under a title.
It may remain this way unless
Your muse comes nudge you a little.

Then you become an instrument,
The sole bearer of her good news,
Hoping that these silent moments,
Of thought sharing she feels enthused.

But don't you worry if ever
From her slumber comes no babble.
Just return over and over
To sit again at the table.

Webcam

I saw you yesterday
It was such a delight,
You appeared should I say,
Like a dream made aright.

Your smile of daring kid
Was stunning but perplex'.
Your gestures though timid
Reflected all your texts.

So I looked at you there
So close and yet so far,
I could not help but stare
At my future bright star.

You were tailor made for
These my arms to surround
A long, long time before
You came down to this ground.

Thank you for the trouble
That allowed me to see,
Quickly, on a double,
Your sweet face, my chérie.

Babe

I promised I would pray
For love to come my way…
And then came you

I promised I would love
The way my Lord above
Taught me to do.

For gazing in your eyes
I deeply realize'
My dreams came true.

Silently then I say
To the Lord whom I pray
Merci beaucoup.

Stress-free

One of these days I'll look at you
And see the girl for whom I yearn.
One of these days, gray or clear blue,
Your lovely face I will discern.

The painful bridge you're now crossing
Requires of you a stiff toll.
You're taking it but your sighing
Attests your strife; mind against soul.

It's never the end of the world;
This I want you to remember.
Life takes its course and will unfurl
Whether you're awake or slumber.

What is written will come to be
Despite all attempts to hold on.
So let go and let God and see
The bright sun at your horizon.

I wish you the best in your life,
This never ending give and take.
If of turmoil it is so rife
It's to best teach you what's at stake.

You live and learn, so do the same,
Soon your troubles will be all gone.
Don't lose hope and call on His Name
Thus far He has failed to help none.

One of these day I'll see my boo,
As beautiful as she can be.
One of these days I'll come to you
When you're dilemmas will all flee.

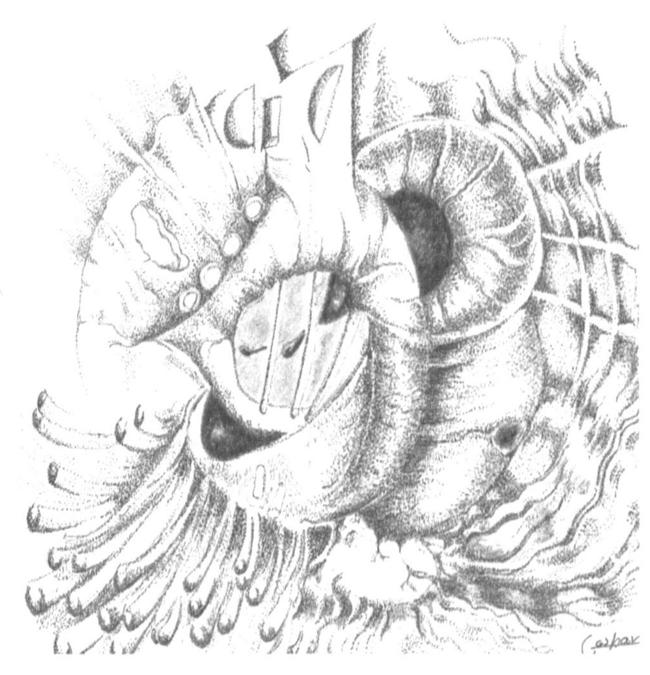

The Thing About Music...

Just like the sun, the air we breathe,
Without music we could not live.
Only to humble souls who pray
Its hidden treasures are displayed.

Music's the food of every soul,
Music's the core of every whole.
Music's the bond given to us
That day language divided us.

Music strengthens the faint of heart,
Gently mends what's broken apart,
Makes us willing, makes us able;
Without music the world crumbles.

There is something about music
That blows away, leaves ecstatic.
It comes to us in many forms.
The least state of mind it reforms.

The elite few who understand
It's origin and don't pretend
To have the power to create
Can tell you much on the debate.

The Father with divine wisdom,
To lighten crosses that may come,
Bequeaths us with its melody
To show the depths of His Mercy.

The blessed ones who right at birth
Grab a hold of its immense worth
Are from the same, very same pod
Of these angels hand made by God.

They come to earth with the purpose
To give spirits their divine dose
Of food needed for their journey
Though belittled by so many.

For from the channels the good Lord
Shows us His great miséricorde,
A musician's the very first
To quench of all souls the deep thirst.

It's known that every time on earth
A musician is given birth,
For having lost one of their race,
Sad tears roll down from angels' face.

But when from us one takes his leave
His soul gladly they come retrieve.
Since the heavens for his soul yearn'
They all rejoice at his return…

The rapture of a melody
Riding a subtle harmony,
Sustained by some ingenious beat;
That can stir up any spirit.

Right there you can ride on cloud nine
Or go caress angels' hair fine.
But if you stand rather than sit
You can be jumping off your feet.

For every song upon this earth
Regardless of how far's its turf,
The impression of any piece
Reflects the muse of the artist.

The true sense of the creation
Maybe lacking stimulation
But it will find a crowd to please,
Certain spirits to put at ease.

Though we disregard the content,
Distaste the artist's real intent
The piece will still find an audience
Willing to savor its essence…

I can never, will never cease
My Creator to try to please.….
No wonder singing to the Lord
Is praying twice with divine chord.

www.ingramcontent.com/pod-product-compliance
Lightning Source LLC
Chambersburg PA
CBHW020544160726
47991CB00002B/571